Ties That Bind

Family and Community

══════════ ✳ ══════════

Published in cooperation with the Denver Museum of Natural History

Series Editor
Beth Steinhorn
Anthropology Educator,
Denver Museum of Natural History

Series Consultants
Betsy R. Armstrong
Director of Publications,
Denver Museum of Natural History

Robert Pickering, Ph.D.
Chair, Department of Anthropology,
Denver Museum of Natural History

Ties That Bind

Family and Community

By
Rebecca Clay

BLACKBIRCH PRESS, INC.
WOODBRIDGE, CONNECTICUT

✳ On the cover: A Malaysian family crowds together on a motorbike (© Nicholas DeVore/Tony Stone Worldwide).

✳ On the title page: An extended family gathers on the steps of a temple in Padjur, India (© David Austen/Tony Stone Worldwide).

Published by Blackbirch Press, Inc.
260 Amity Road
Woodbridge, CT 06525

©1996 Blackbirch Press, Inc.

Printed in Hong Kong.

10 9 8 7 6 5 4 3 2 1

Blackbirch Press, Inc.

Editorial Director: Bruce S. Glassman
Editor: Lisa Clyde Nielsen
Production Editor: Laura E. Specht
Photo Research: Ellen Cibula

Denver Museum of Natural History:

Research Assistant: Carol R. Weiskopf
Photo Archivist: Liz Clancy
Administrative Assistant: Mary Bushbaum

Library of Congress Cataloging-in-Publication Data

Clay, Rebecca, 1956–
     Ties that bind: family / by Rebecca Clay. — 1st ed.
          p.   cm. — (Our human family)
     "Published in cooperation with the Denver Museum of Natural History"
     Includes bibliographical references and index.
     ISBN 1–56711–126–2 (lib. bdg.)
     1. Family—Juvenile literature. 2. Family—Cross-cultural studies—Juvenile literature. I. Denver Museum of Natural History. II. Title. III. Series.
HQ515.C53   1995
306.85—dc20
                                                                    94–46632
                                                                    CIP

Contents

Introduction

As we neared the end of an exciting journey through Turkey, my traveling companion and I stood at the back of a commuter ferry and sailed up the Bosporus Strait, away from the capital city of Istanbul. As the boat chugged away, we soaked up the comforting sight of the cozy three- and four-story row houses that lined the shores. The ferry zigzagged across the narrow Bosporus, stopping frequently to unload passengers, and we caught sight of two young girls staring wide-eyed at us. Both my friend and I immediately assumed the girls were sisters—their matching brown hair and deep brown eyes gave them away. The older one—about thirteen—smiled and, without saying a word, held out a crumpled bag of pistachio nuts in a universal gesture of friendship. Tickled, my friend and I accepted and, in return, offered the girls a handful of chocolate candy we kept stashed in our packs for just such an occasion.

Over the next hour, we and many other passengers were entertained as the girls presided over a floating language classroom, designed to teach us the essentials of Turkish: *lüften* ("please"), *feribot* ("ferry"), and, of course, *fistik* ("pistachio nut"). They also offered a small geography lesson as they pointed out their town on the map. In return, we pulled out a map and pointed to our towns—worlds away, or so it seemed. Soon the younger sister—about seven—took my hand and led us down below to where a group of women were unpacking lunches from their bags. We did our best to introduce ourselves, stumbling in Turkish, laughing a little, smiling a lot. Clearly these were our young friends' mothers and aunts—and they were as friendly and gracious as could be. By the time the ferry approached their stop, my companion and I had relished tastes of dates, figs, and börek—the popular and tasty spinach pastries. In return, they had enjoyed listening to our small gifts of American jazz tapes. Before we parted, we exchanged addresses so that we could send copies of the pictures we had taken of each other. Finally, as all good mothers would, the women made sure that my friend and I knew which bus to take back to the city. They even gave us bus tickets in case we didn't have the correct coins.

As we rode back to Istanbul, I marveled at how two groups of people from such disparate cultures could meet and, in just an hour, bridge oceans of differences in order to become friends. How had we managed—with so few words and common experiences— to communicate, laugh, share lunch, and even decide that we actually liked each other? A few years later—on a beach halfway around the world—another encounter brought these thoughts rushing back.

It was during an expedition to the cold, foggy tip of a Siberian peninsula that I met other children, this time gathered, curious, as we stepped off our boat and onto the rocky beach of their small village. A few adults stood watching, more cautious, at the edge of a cluster of grey, peeling buildings that were barely visible from shore.

As I stood facing a handful of ten- to twelve-year-old Siberian boys, I was immediately struck by the obstacles that seemed to stand between us: We didn't speak the same language; we knew virtually nothing about each other; and we had only a few hours before our ship continued its journey northbound.

Our first attempts at communication were the obvious hand signals and smiles, but we met little success. Then one of the boys discreetly pulled a small hidden treasure from his pocket, and the others quickly followed suit. Within seconds, our group was presented with a wonderful variety of items, including a collection of carved animals in bone and ivory, small leather pouches trimmed with seal fur, and a rock of a particularly interesting shape. All these treasures were being held out to us for sale or trade, a universal language that all my fellow travelers understood immediately.

Meanwhile, one boy pulled me aside and proudly demonstrated his handmade sling shot. As he aimed at a fence, cans on the beach, and an unfortunate team of dogs chained to a nearby post, he gave me a no-frills lesson in Siberian sling-shot technique.

It had been only twenty or thirty minutes since our arrival, but by the time we all walked up the beach together, we had become at least short-term friends. When we reached town, the boys enthusiastically introduced us to their families. Naturally, we took out photos of our families and offered views in return. We then traded a few modest trinkets and, before we departed, were given a guided tour of the village museum. There we caught glimpses of the spectacular ivory carvings that make the artists of this particular village famous.

In both the bustling outskirts of Istanbul and the remote Siberian village, I came face to face with young people from worlds vastly different from my own. In each case, we were separated by different languages, customs, and lifestyles. Both times, however, curiosity, a desire to learn, and a shared sense of friendship, family, and fun enabled us to bring our worlds together for a brief time.

The memories I have of Turkey and Siberia—as well as others like them—come to my mind often as I work in museums, study anthropology collections, and teach others about cultures. These are recollections I hold particularly dear because, above all, they remind me of what it really means to be human. They prove that, even though people may appear very different on the surface, our differences all grow out of the same basic needs. They grow out of needs that all humans share: the need to communicate; to create and appreciate beauty; to learn; even the need to play and have fun.

All of these needs connect us. What makes us different is how each group of people develops its own unique answers to these needs. Together, their answers create a unique way of life, a pattern we call culture. But, underneath the patterns on the surface—whether we live in a big-city apartment or dwell in a desert tent—we remain linked by our common needs. These needs, and the human spirit that enables us to fulfill them, bind us together into one "human family."

Beth Steinhorn
Anthropology Educator
Denver Museum of Natural History

1

Families Are Everywhere

What do you think when you think of a human family? You probably start by picturing your own family, maybe a mother and father, brothers and sisters, aunts and uncles, cousins or grandparents. You may also imagine relatives who live in another town, state, or even a distant country. And what about the people who aren't directly related to you but whom everyone considers a part of your family?

Families are everywhere; they are in your neighborhood, in your community, and in every region of the world. Families hunt together in the icy Arctic, roam together across the hot Sahara, and run errands together on busy city streets. They may travel far to visit each other on special family occasions, to share the joys of a wedding or the birth of a newborn child, or mourn the death of a grandparent. Families are groups of people, young and old, who are forever bonded by blood, love, and the need to survive.

* Opposite: The men of an Israeli family rejoice in a bar mitzvah ceremony at the Western Wall in Jerusalem.

Although all families share certain common bonds, family structures often differ, depending on several key factors. Two of the most important factors are where a family lives and how its members support themselves. For example, does the family live in a rain forest or a huge industrial city? Are they rice farmers or do they sell automobiles? Are they nomadic or firmly settled in one region? Do they have access to education, training, and employment? These are a few of the factors that help determine a family's structure and make it unique.

More important than what makes families different is what makes them alike. Whether rich or poor, well-educated or illiterate, each family in the world shares the same basic universal functions and needs. No matter where they live or what language they speak, no matter how large or small, all families share a common human heritage.

A family is a group of related people who, together, are responsible for a number of basic functions. First, a family creates and cares for its children. Second, it teaches its young what it means to be a productive and responsible member of society. Third, a family shares work and fun together. And fourth, a family shares in the care of its elderly members. A closer look at these four family cornerstones will provide a greater understanding of the ways in which families function around the world.

Caring for Children

Parents are usually the family members who take primary care of their children, but other family members may share that responsibility. For example, grandparents may help raise children and watch them while parents work. In some agrarian-based (agricultural) societies in Africa, young sons move away from their parents to live with their mother's brother and inherit some of his land. In this case, the boy's uncle takes care of him while the boy's father takes on the role of a friend.

Families give their children the security they need to grow up and become healthy and productive members of society.

Within the family, children are loved and cared for, fed and clothed, and protected from danger. Without the safety and affection of the family, very few children would survive the many dangers of the world.

Teaching the Young

Communities and families function best when they share common values and rules. Family members will often teach each other what it means to be a member of a group or community. Grown family members usually teach the children how best to behave toward other children and adults. They also let them know which duties and responsibilities children in their society are expected to fulfill. Some cultures, such as many Native-American societies and African societies, teach values through the ancient art of storytelling. This tradition passes down cultural wisdom orally from one generation to the next.

In most cultures, children learn the basic social rules from their elders. In

✳ A grandfather shows his grandson how to tend a garden in Siberia, Russia.

Japan, children must understand that their society's system determines each person's status by age and sex. The older one is, the more respect he or she is given. Young Japanese children also learn that they may have to sacrifice their own individual needs for the greater welfare of their family and community. These children are prepared for their roles in society by learning such traditional rules and values.

Like Japan, certain cultures of South America also place a great deal of importance on the societal values of cooperation and sharing. Among the Mundurucu people of Brazil, children learn the most important social value of traditional Mundurucu society: that they must cooperate with each other and share everything. When Mundurucu children grow up, they teach their own children this same basic rule.

* A family of fishermen pulls in its nets at sunset in Acapulco, Mexico.

Sharing Work and Fun

Some kids do chores at night or on the weekends to help keep their homes clean and organized. That's one common way children work to help their families. In many societies, families also hunt, gather, farm, build houses, make clothing and blankets, and prepare meals together.

And after the work is finished, the fun can begin. During leisure times, young people often play games and sports while the adults share jokes and laughter. Many families also come together to dance and play music during parties and major celebrations such as birthdays and weddings. Having fun is an important way for families to stay happy and to celebrate the joy they feel in their unique kind of togetherness.

Caring for the Elderly

When elderly family members can no longer take care of themselves, children, grandchildren, and other relatives make sure the needs of the elders are met. In some societies, the elderly live with their children's family as soon as that family is created. If not, they may move in with younger family members in order to be better taken care of.

In the same way that families provide security for their young, they also create a safe place for their elderly. In China, for example, younger family members are responsible for the primary care of their elderly parents and grandparents. In the United States, it is not as common for the elderly to move in with, and be cared for by, their children at home. Instead, older grandparents may live in a retirement community or nursing home where they have access to care from professional nurses and doctors.

Whether or not they live with their older children, most elderly parents and grandparents are respected by their families. They remember that their own survival and happiness depended on the care they received as children from those loving and nurturing relatives.

Marriage Creates Families

Marriage provides a key framework for the creation and care of children. A husband and wife begin a new branch of their two families by creating or adopting children.

Marriages also solidify alliances within communities and between different cultural groups. In some societies, a bride and groom may have barely met before they say their wedding vows. In this case, they are not marrying for love but, rather, to unite two families and bring together new sources of labor and land. Such marriages may be arranged by the parents, and each family

✳ The bride and groom of a Japanese wedding party pose proudly for a portrait in Toyohashi.

expects to profit from the alliance by becoming larger, wealthier, and more powerful.

Some traditional cultures have developed the practice of polygyny, in which a man may have more than one wife (often sisters) at a time. Other societies have developed polyandry, in which a woman can marry more than one man (often brothers). These variations in family structure are often accepted because they are critical to the family's survival and success. Among the Tiwi of Australia, for example, polygamy allows a family to prosper through the combined agricultural work of several women in one household. It also enables young women to benefit from the skills and knowledge of the older women. The older wives, for example, teach the younger ones how to find edible plants and hunt small animals.

In most industrial societies, however, including the United States, people are allowed to marry only one person at a time. They can, however, take a new spouse if their husband or wife dies or if the marriage is dissolved by divorce. Having only one spouse at a time is called serial monogamy. If adults with children remarry, a new kind of family—called a stepfamily or a blended family—is created.

Kinship Is Not Just Being Genetically Related

"Kinship" refers to people who are related or formally bonded together in some way. In many cultures, kinship systems are complex, interwoven structures with very defined rules. In other cultures, kinships are based more on family traditions or common practices. Kinship systems differ from one society to another. In many industrialized countries, for example, an unrelated godparent may be asked to be responsible for a child's spiritual life. Among the Inuit of Alaska, some couples even create a "double marriage" with another couple, to make sure their children would be well cared for if something happened to the biological parents.

A group of people who have a shared identity and property and trace their descent from a common ancestor is called a clan. Clans are common family structures worldwide, most notably in

✻ Members of a Masai tribe in Kenya relax together.

Native-American cultures as well as among other peoples who trace their roots to tribal societies.

Some families hardly distinguish among members who are related genetically, by marriage, or by kinship association. For example, you may call your mother's sister "aunt" in the same way that you call your mother's brother's wife "aunt," even though one is related biologically and the other is related by marriage. The Chinese take this approach even further: Children in China call every adult female in the community *ayi*, or "aunt," and they call every adult male *shushu*, or "uncle." And in the African country of Sudan, people in the Nuer tribe address those much older than they as "mother" and "father," those the same age as "brother" and "sister," and those much younger as "daughter" and "son," regardless of any actual genetic or kinship relation.

A Family Doesn't Have to Live Together to Be a Family

Entire families rarely live under the same roof or even in the same community. Young family members in rural settings, for example, often leave the countryside for better educational or job opportunities in the city. Others abandon the city for a quieter life in the suburbs. In the United States, family members are often spread out across the country and communicate by telephone calls and letters, getting together once or twice a year on holidays.

Having family members in distant regions also creates kinship networks. Such networks can help people migrate from place to place, as occurs in Africa. With a sister or an uncle living in the city, a young Nigerian man may more easily leave his family village for a new job in the country's capital, Lagos. Without such a family tie, the newcomer may have a much harder time getting established amid millions of strangers.

Families Are Different Within Each Society

The basic needs and functions of a family are universal, yet each culture has its own vision of the ideal family. But real families don't always fit that ideal. The family structure that best helps a family prosper within its particular environment is usually considered the ideal. In China and many other Asian cultures, for example, the ideal family has usually meant that all generations live under one roof. But what is ideal for one generation may not be ideal for the next. Just as cultures change, so does their concept of the ideal family.

In the United States, the traditional "nuclear" family has been a married couple living with its biological children and no one else. But this situation is no longer typical. Today, one of every two children lives in a different kind of family, including families with single parents. Many homes are now multigenerational, with a grandparent helping to raise the children. Other families are "blended," with a combination of stepparents, stepchildren, and half-siblings. In other households, children may live with two parents who are not married.

✳ A young Machiguenga mother holds her baby outside their home in the Andes Mountains of Peru.

Margaret Mead, the famous anthropologist, once said that "the task of each family is also the task of all humanity. This is to cherish the living, remember those who have gone before, and prepare for those who are not yet born."

Cultures change over time. Yet despite change, people's sense of family remains the most important tie that binds them together. It is a universal social unit that serves our physical and emotional needs. As social, economic, and political arrangements develop, evolve, and even collapse, we all still need to be part of a stable and caring family. This need joins all cultures, making us, in many ways, one big human family.

2

*T*he Americas

The Americas stretch from high in the arctic tundra of northern Canada down to the rocky Cape Horn on the tip of South America. Over the centuries, the physical environment of each distinctive region has helped to shape the cultural traditions of the human families that live and work there. Many North, Central, and South American peoples are descended from Europeans, Africans, or Asians, as well as from indigenous (native) groups. They have gradually combined their native customs with those of other cultures present in the so-called New World.

As they have in the past, some indigenous peoples still rely on local natural resources to feed and clothe themselves. In the far north, for example, some members of the Inuit community

21

✳ Opposite: The children of an Amish family gather together on the steps of their home in Pennsylvania, United States.

still hunt caribou and sea mammals. Near the equator and in the rain forests, native peoples harvest tropical fruits and nuts using the techniques of their ancestors. And along the coast-lines, fishermen continue to count on the seas for their families' sustenance, just as generations before them have.

Over the last 150 years, many regions in North, Central, and South America have been industrialized and urbanized. In the United States and the lower regions of Canada, for example, this means that family life often revolves around office or facto-ry jobs and commuting from suburban homes to city skyscrapers. Industrialized societies tend to have smaller nuclear families, with one or two children, and each family occupies a home away from other family members, such as grandparents, aunts, and uncles.

In industrialized societies, federal and local governments also set up public school systems that educate and train the youngest citizens. In this way the government shares the burden of preparing the young to become productive members of society, rather than leaving this responsibility entirely to the family. In industrialized democracies, voters elect national, state, and local officials to develop the laws that will influence community and family life.

Caring for Children

Because of the many different ethnic and economic groups found in the region, families and childrearing techniques in the Americas vary greatly from one region to the next. For exam-ple, some indigenous groups in South and Central America keep their children at home and raise them to hunt or farm as their ancestors did. Parents in industrialized cultures, however, such as those in Canada and the United States, often leave the majority of their children's care and education to professional caregivers and educators. Indigenous families often raise their children to rely on, and be responsible for, the long-term care of other family members. Many urban children in North America, though, are taught to be independent and self-sufficient.

❋ A young Inuit boy is given a lesson in ice fishing from his father on Holman Island, Canada.

Different cultures also have varying approaches to discipline in order to achieve their ends. Inuit children, for example, are rarely scolded or directly disciplined. Their parents believe severe punishment would be both immoral and ineffective. Instead, they consider gentle steering the best recipe for good behavior. But rather than become spoiled, by the time they are ten years old, many children have already begun to assume mature duties, including fishing, trapping, and hunting. That means they are expected to begin contributing to the family's food supply as soon as they are able.

Similarly, among the Cree of Quebec, Canada, parents rarely tell their children what to do; instead, they teach by providing an example. They call this kind of child-raising practice "shadowing." Rather than directing a child to go outside and chop wood, for instance, the father will do it himself. Over time, he expects the child to follow or "shadow" him; that is, to watch and learn how to do it correctly.

Many urban North American parents also attempt to instill values in their children by setting examples to follow. The difference between their approach and that of the Inuit or Cree, however, is that these parents often use systems of reward and punishment as integral parts of their childrearing practices in addition to setting examples.

Systems of caring for children also vary according to culture and to urban versus rural settings. In many urban, middle-class North American families, both parents work away from home and the children spend much of the day at school or in day care. This separation of home and business affects how often family members can work on common projects. In addition, some married couples put off having children until they feel emotionally and financially prepared. Other couples may decide not to have children at all, preferring to focus all their time and energy on their professional lives instead.

When they divorce, some North American couples share the custody of, or legal responsibility for, their children. For example, a child may spend three days a week with her father, and the other four with her mother. If the parents marry again, the children may acquire a stepparent and stepsiblings. In fact, such children may suddenly inherit a whole new stepfamily!

Even though female-based child care is the norm in much of the world, in more rural American settings it is not uncommon for fathers to play an active role in the daily care of children.

✳ A group of children listens quietly during story time at a day-care center in New York City, United States.

In the farming and fishing village of Grande Anse on the northern coast of Trinidad in the Caribbean, for example, some fathers actively participate in the daily care of their infants and young children. Although mothers do most of the work, fathers also hold, feed, clean, and play with the children, as well as change their diapers. Because many extended families live under one roof, children also receive a lot of attention from aunts, uncles, and grandparents.

✳ A Peruvian mother sits bundled tightly with her infant as her daughter helps with care.

In the Andean community of Uchucmarca in northern Peru, there is safety in numbers, and families rely on kinship for their survival. Family members develop close bonds so the basic needs of children and the elderly can be taken care of without much trouble. But when children grow up and marry, they often prefer to establish separate households of their own, sometimes in the same neighborhood or in an extended-family compound.

Teaching Values to the Young

Many native peoples in North, Central, and South America believe their cultural and spiritual values were shaped by the natural forces of their environment—including the winds, rivers, seas, mountains, and plains. Through oral traditions such as storytelling, they pass on these beliefs to their children. Included in these tales are messages about the group's cultural values, such as the importance of sharing and giving. These stories also teach children early on how to combine their spiritual beliefs with the values needed for daily living.

✳ A girl poses with her family after her First Communion ceremony in Flores, Guatemala.

    In traditional Inuit families, the mother is often responsible for teaching cultural values to her children. As her mother once did, she teaches her children the ritual ceremonies of thanking and showing respect to the land and animals on which they rely for survival. She may show them, for example, what part of an animal the hunter has to return to the earth, in order to ensure more animals in the years to come.

    Gwich'in families of the Alaskan Arctic teach their children the importance of caribou to human survival. They learn how to use every part of the animal, so nothing is wasted. Elders also teach younger family members that by taking care of the tundra, the tundra will in turn take care of them.

Like the Inuit and Gwich'in, many other children in the United States and Canada learn their social values and customs from family members and from the community at large. In addition to learning from parents, children may turn to school teachers and even television programs to help determine what is expected of them. Young adults also learn the importance of education, hard work, and financial success from their elders.

Preparing for the future is an important part of Navajo life as well. Navajo children are taught that the thoughts, words, and actions of the people who live today will have an effect on people born seven generations from now. Therefore, all Navajo family members must consider the impact of their decisions on their descendants a century later.

Sharing Work and Fun

In North America, many young people leave home as older teenagers to attend college or to find work. Their first jobs may take them far away from their hometowns, to a different city or state. They may even marry someone who grew up thousands of miles away or in another country. Throughout much of North America, it is not uncommon for siblings to live hundreds or thousands of miles from each other and from parents and grandparents. In this case, they may take an airplane to see each other on a special occasion, such as a wedding or funeral. The rest of the time they may keep in touch through greeting cards, letters, and talking on the telephone.

In many indigenous, agrarian-based societies, however, families tend to live and work within the same region. Among the Cree of Quebec, a father may take his young son to hunt geese in the same area where his own father took him when he was a boy. It is also common for an older male family member, such as an uncle, to share a hunting spot with his nephew, and pass it on to him when he dies. After the hunt, family and friends may share a sweat lodge together. By sharing the intense heat created by hot rocks, the group acknowledges that all the members are related.

✳ A mother and her daughters work together sorting grain in Oaxaca, Mexico.

Like the Cree, the Navajo elders transmit important skills and information to the youngest generation. Many Navajo girls study the secrets of tribal medicine with their grandmothers. Female family members often know which plants to use to treat for different illnesses. Today, many Native-American women are also political leaders and activists, seeking new ways to help their tribes not only survive but thrive.

Children in Central American farming villages often work side by side with their parents, growing corn and beans, picking coffee beans, and harvesting sugarcane. In Mexico, it may be the children's job to watch the donkeys and pigs while their mothers raise flowers and fruit. In communities near the border, husbands and fathers often leave home to work in the United States. These men—called *braceros*—send a portion of their earnings home to help supplement their family's income.

Families in the Uchucmarca Valley of northern Peru often divide family labor along clear sex and age lines. Men and older sons do the heavier agricultural work in the fields while the women stay home to maintain the household. Sometimes the women shepherd the sheep and gather firewood near the village. Mothers also teach their daughters how to spin and weave, as well as cook and prepare food.

Caring for the Elderly

Many families in industrialized areas are not able to easily care for their elderly parents and grandparents, often because of the demands of work and children and limited living space. In this case, it is common for senior citizens to continue to live alone or in a retirement community if they are still in good health. Because these elderly people, like their children, have been raised to be self-sufficient, many prefer to be on their own for as long as possible. If they get sick, however, close family members try to find the best way to care for them.

In African-American culture—even though many elderly live on their own—it is a tradition for large families to get together for the birthdays of elderly family members, such as a great-grandmother or great-great-great aunt. For the event, the many "kindred" who make up the family travel to the family's hometown. Even frail senior citizens often live alone and take care of themselves with the help of children, grandchildren, and friends who live nearby.

✴ African-American cousins play dominoes together during a big family reunion in Texas, United States.

Among the Native-American cultures, the elderly are both cared for and revered. Special respect is given because they have lived the longest and in those years have collected important wisdom they can share with younger family members. And sometimes family elders are the only ones who remember family history, traditional customs, and even their native language. For this reason, many Native-American families try to make sure that their elderly share their knowledge and experience with the next generations.

Among the Eskimos of Alaska, ancestors are so revered that each newborn child is named after an old relative, often a grandparent, whom the parent wants to immortalize. This name, or *atiq*, is very important to a person's status and identity. It is common even for strangers to ask each other which relative they were named after.

In many Native-American families, ancestral traditions have been lost through acculturation, meaning the change of one culture through the strong influence of another. Today, young Native-American men and women throughout North America are looking to their older relatives to help bring back lost languages, arts, and religious practices. As keepers of the culture, the elders represent an irreplaceable source of information for their descendants.

✳ A young father holds his daughter proudly at a Native-American cultural festival in Canada.

Families Change

Because much of North America is highly industrialized and many

✳ A single-parent mother shows her daughter how to feed chickens on a farm in New Hampshire, United States.

regions depend on urban settings for their economic survival, family members have scattered across the continent, often settling down far from their hometowns. Partly because of the constantly changing needs of the industrialized workplace, divorce in North America has become more common than in many other parts of the world. Some couples choose to divorce after several years of marriage, and, when they do, their family structure changes significantly. In those cases, children may be raised by just one parent, rather than two. Despite the popular bias against single-parent families, many such children grow up to be just as happy and successful as they would have in a more traditional two-parent setting. This is just one example of how families can have shapes and sizes that are different from the ideal, and still provide the love, comfort, and security that all human beings profoundly want and need. The beauty of most family structures is that they can change and adapt to many circumstances without sacrificing their most basic ability to care for their members.

3

Africa

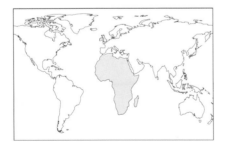

Africa is a huge continent of greatly varying climates, landscapes, ethnic groups, languages, and lifestyles. Its many nations stretch from the Mediterranean Sea, above the equator, to the Cape of Good Hope, on the tip of South Africa. From vast, harsh deserts to dense rain forests and majestic mountains, many African people still live and work in ways similar to their ancestors. Many are still hunter-gatherers, pastoralists (herders), or farmers, but today increasing numbers of Africa's youth are migrating to cities to take jobs in offices and factories.

Most African countries were colonized by one European power or another during the 1800s. (The British, French, Portuguese, and Dutch were the major colonizers.) Over time,

✳ Opposite: A nomadic mother from Sudan spins wool as her child sleeps in a portable bed.

✳ A village chief poses with his fourteen wives in Khor Machi, Sudan.

the traditional cultures of the area became influenced by new languages and traditions of the powers that ruled there. This European influence was historically strongest in the cities, which means many urban dwellers have forgotten or never learned the ways of their ancestors.

In Lagos, the capital of Nigeria, for example, many city dwellers now reject traditional marriage customs in favor of Western-style church weddings with white veils and multitiered wedding cakes. Many savanna tribes, on the other hand—including the Masai of East Africa, and the !Kung Bushmen of Southern Africa—continue to practice traditional family rituals, in large part due to their relative isolation.

Caring for Children

Because living conditions can be harsh, not all African children live until puberty or even past infancy. Although a mother may give birth to numerous children, only a few of them may survive. This is one reason why a number of African societies practice polygyny; each additional wife means more workers and more children who boost the husband's wealth and status in the community. In a hunter-gatherer society, each wife also provides more food by accompanying the other women into the bush to find plants and fruits.

In Nigeria, a Muslim man is allowed to have up to four wives if he can treat and care for them equally. Among the !Kung, on the other hand, only about five percent of the men prefer two wives to one. The second wife helps extend her husband's social and political influence to include her family, her village, and their foraging grounds. But although the first wife's position in the family usually remains the strongest, many !Kung women today do not want their husbands to marry others. Jealousy and rivalry among co-wives can make polygynous life difficult and even intolerable.

!Kung children are almost never separated from their mothers during their first few years. They are toted around all through the day, either wrapped around their mother's hip in a sling or toddling around at her feet. Even if she travels far to seek food for the family, a !Kung mother will bring her children along. Because they traditionally give birth only once every three to four years, !Kung women also lavish each child with a long period of exclusive attention, which they believe enhances the child's sense of security and well-being.

Teaching Values to the Young

Since many rural African children do not go to school, they learn their values from their families at home. Many important lessons and values are transmitted through a rich oral tradition. At night, Masai elders tell ancient stories and folktales that emphasize the tribe's longstanding social rules. These stories often highlight the importance of friendship—without which many Masai may not survive the savanna's many dangers—and the importance of work, which keeps the family fed and housed. Masai children also learn to show respect for their elders. For example, when greeting an older person, they are taught to bow and wait to be touched on the head before speaking.

Family stories also help children gain a sense of pride in their history and culture. Zulu children in South Africa learn their society's history and values from their grandmothers, who have often become great storytellers over the years. Young people hear about the heroic adventures of their ancestors, which, in turn, inspires them to behave in a similar way.

In the primarily Islamic countries of North Africa, children learn the rules and values of society at home and at school. Religion plays an integral role in the rituals of daily life. Every day, each child must read the Koran, the Muslim holy book, which contains strict laws about what behavior is and is not acceptable. While reading the Koran, girls learn that when they approach womanhood, they will most likely begin to wear a veil over their face, for modesty, just as Muslim women have done for centuries.

Sharing Work and Fun

In many African communities, children are essential members whose labor helps the family survive. The division of chores within the family is often clearly defined. In hunter-gatherer societies, many boys learn to hunt with their fathers, while it is common for girls to find out from their mothers where the best plants, berries, and nuts can be found.

Around the age of twelve, !Kung boys traditionally receive a bow and a set of arrows from their fathers and learn to shoot birds and rabbits. Later, they will follow their

✳ A young Masai family poses in front of its home in the Loita Hills of rural Kenya.

✳ A family works together to draw water from a well near Nara, Mali.

fathers, uncles, and older brothers into the bush to hunt large animals. When the meat is brought back to the village, it is distributed according to each hunter's kinship and his contribution to the kill. The hunters also tell exciting stories about the chase to family members who stayed behind.

In pastoralist communities, the older children must watch over their younger brothers and sisters, help with the cooking and cleaning, tend the family's domestic animals, and go to the market with their mothers. In a Masai family, it is also the women's and girls' job to milk the cows. The family women keep the huts in good condition by patching them regularly with fresh cow dung. While the girls collect firewood and get water for eating and washing, the boys herd the animals toward the grazing area, which can be dangerous because it is often far from home where lions also roam.

Caring for the Elderly

As they do in most societies, grandparents play an important role in African families, because they are the oldest and have lived the longest. Grandparents are admired for being the wisest and most experienced in life. They also often have more time to play with the children and listen to their concerns. Alternate generations provide a special relationship in !Kung

✳ Three generations of a Burundi family pose for a portrait near the center of their village.

families, especially if the child is a grandparent's "namesake." Sometimes !Kung children—like children in many other cultures—feel they can express their feelings more easily to their grandparents.

As a !Kung ages, he or she receives more and more respect from younger family and community members. But because of the harshness of African savanna life, relatively few !Kung survive into old age. Those who do are often in excellent health, though they can no longer work hard. The !Kung cannot avoid becoming dependent on their children and grandchildren, which is fine because !Kung are raised to share all their resources. In this society, the elderly are secure in knowing their basic needs will be met. At the same time, they contribute to their children and community by providing information and wisdom, explaining the family's history, or knowing where to locate food in times of scarcity.

Families Change

In recent years, rural African families have begun to get smaller. Large families are still preferred in many ways, but today that traditional social value is starting to disappear, in great part because of economic pressures. Rapidly rising populations in Africa are cutting into the amount of land on which a family can farm, raise livestock, or hunt and gather. With less land, a family does not need the extra labor that a new child provides, nor can it afford the additional mouth to feed.

Because of economic difficulties in many rural communities, a large number of Africans are gradually migrating to the big cities. This means families are often split between urban and rural dwellers. When young people leave their childhood villages, they usually go where they already have relatives. This way, they have people who can support them emotionally and financially through the transition. As in many rural African families, when Zulu men leave their homes to find work in the cities, they leave their wives to manage on their own. When the men find a job on a sugar plantation or a construction site, for example, they live in work hostels and send money.

The Effect of Politics

Until the early 1990s, in South Africa, black families were confined to special "homelands" that the white government established. Now the system of apartheid (racial separateness) has been abolished and the country has an integrated leadership, so families can move around more easily. This mobility means that many families are separating and dispersing for the first time. The long-term effect that this will have on family structures, traditions, and communication remains to be seen.

Some African families are also divided by oceans and continents. Wealthy Africans often send their children abroad to study at foreign universities, in countries where some students eventually settle. In this way, many more African families are spreading out across the globe. Young students are absorbing new influences from diverse cultures and offering others an opportunity to become familiar with the unique aspects of their African heritage.

✳ Urban South Africans hustle their way to work near the State Theatre in downtown Pretoria.

4

Europe and the Middle East

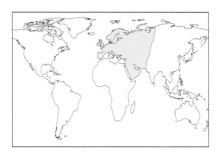

The families of Europe and the Middle East are as varied as the languages they speak and the customs they practice. Europe includes the United Kingdom, Scandinavia, Ireland, continental Western Europe, Eastern Europe, and European Russia. Southeast of Europe is the Middle East, which includes Israel and many Arab countries. The ancient civilizations of the Middle East cradled the development of much of Europe's civilization.

Many Europeans and Middle Easterners to this day work in traditional professions, such as agriculture and tending livestock. They grow fruits and vegetables, and raise cows, sheep, goats,

41

✳ Opposite: A Bedouin father rests in the shade with his child while traveling through the Syrian desert, near Talt.

and pigs for regional and global markets. Some make a living from fishing, primarily in the Atlantic Ocean, Mediterranean Sea, and Persian Gulf. Others work in office jobs in the big cities, such as Milan, Cairo, Tel Aviv, and London. There are engineers, computer programmers, accountants, businesspeople, and every other kind of professional. In the Middle East, traditional sheiks and nomads, who exist alongside a growing middle class, call the oil-rich desert their home.

As in most societies, European and Middle Eastern family structures and expectations are shaped in large part by people's spiritual beliefs. Christianity, Islam, and Judaism are the predominant faiths of these two vast regions. Before the collapse of the Soviet Union in 1991, Communist beliefs were the primary influence that shaped family life in Russia and the former Soviet republics. This often meant that societal duties, as determined by the central government, took priority over the individual needs of family life. As more democratic forms of government have taken hold, families in the former Soviet Union have focused more attention on personal needs and have been free to make more choices for themselves.

Caring for Children

European family life has been profoundly affected by the development of technology over the years. Because of products such as refrigerators, dishwashers, and washing machines, women in

✳ A day-care worker presides over nap time at the Lokki Day Care Center in Helsinki, Finland.

recent years have had less housework and more free time. This means that many women now work outside of the home and spend less time taking care of their children.

Since many mothers now have full-time jobs that may require going to an office every weekday, their infants and toddlers often spend the hours between breakfast and dinner in day-care centers. For example, in France, the government provides free day care for babies as young as two months, and after-school care for older children. The workers at these centers play an important role in helping French families raise their children, by teaching the young ones how to play and cooperate with each other.

✳ A Russian family travels the snowy streets of Novosibirsk together.

In the evening, mothers or fathers pick the children up from the day-care center and bring them home. At home, the mother often cooks a hot meal on the stove, and later puts the dirty dishes in a dishwasher. Clothes can be easily cleaned in a washing machine or can be sent out. Older children are encouraged to help with such chores. After dinner, the whole family may watch television together or different family members may take turns talking with friends on the telephone.

Having a car allows many European families to be more mobile. That means parents drive their children to soccer or ballet practice, for example, or to visit grandparents in the country. In general, many technological innovations have given families more time to have fun together, rather than spending long hours cooking, cleaning, and getting from one place to the next.

Teaching Values to the Young

Many European and Middle Eastern families learn their values from their religious beliefs. The principal religions are Judaism, Protestantism, Catholicism, Greek Orthodox, and Islam. The core of these beliefs is that everyone must respect each other. Children are taught to obey their parents and elders. Sometimes they are punished, with a lecture or a spanking, for example, to show them the importance of these values.

Most children go to school, where they learn about the history of their nations and their cultures in addition to the values they learn at home. Through this history, they are exposed to the values of their ancestors. They learn about their national heroes and heroines. Schoolchildren in Great Britain, for example, study national icons such as Winston Churchill and William Shakespeare. Students in Egypt study their political leaders, such as Anwar Sadat, and Gamal Abdel Nasser. In many cases, they are also given a civics lesson, which tells them what kind of behavior their society expects of them.

In Ireland, many children go to church with their parents every Sunday. Most Irish people are Catholic, and they try to bring their children up as Catholics as well. As part of this upbringing, many children attend Sunday School, where they

✳ Children take a break for lunch at their Catholic school in Capri, Italy.

Life on a Kibbutz

✳ Play time at the Kibbutz Bet Guvrin in Israel.

In Israel, about 125,000 people live in 270 *kibbutzim*, or rural communes. (Kibbutzim is the plural for kibbutz.) The Hebrew word *kibbutz* loosely means "communal settlement." The first kibbutzim were developed in the mid-1930s by young Jewish pioneers from Eastern Europe, as a way to help establish a permanent Jewish community. Israel is the only country in the world that has these independent communities. Today, most kibbutzim are home to between 400 and 600 adults and children who live and work together, like one big family.

A kibbutz is also a well-organized farm and business that provides all of its own and much of Israel's food and manufactured goods. Each kibbutz is managed by an elected committee that takes care of the residents' basic needs, including education, housing, and entertainment. Before the State of Israel was established in 1948, the kibbutz played an important role in helping immigrants get settled in the area, and in developing the region's agriculture. Today, the kibbutzim still play an important role in Israeli society; for example, they continue to support Jewish culture with musical and theater performances, festivals, and special museums. Many Israelis and Jewish Americans regularly visit and volunteer to work on kibbutzim for short periods of time.

In most kibbutzim, children live in children's houses, spending most of their waking hours with their peers. As they grow older, they move to a new children's house that has facilities for their age. In school, the children are taught the values of cooperation and work. Because the kibbutz takes care of many household duties and responsibilities, parents often have more time to spend time with their children after work and on weekends and holidays.

Kibbutz life in Israel has been changing in recent years. While in the past daily activities were more focused on the community than the family, today kibbutz society is becoming more family-centered and parents are allowed to take more responsibility for their own children's care. Women are also spending less time working and more time with their children. In addition, some people have been leaving the kibbutzim, because they find life there too confining and restrictive. But most choose to stay because of the sense of security in belonging to a small, closed community.

read stories from the Bible. These stories help to teach them important values, such as the difference between right and wrong. They also learn the Bible's Ten Commandments, which offer morals and directions to guide them in their daily behavior.

Religious ceremonies in Ireland, such as the parades on St. Patrick's Day, bring different families in the community together. Before they begin to share a meal, families also say grace together. This is an important ritual that allows everyone to give thanks for the food and for each other.

Greek children are surrounded by the history of their ancient civilization. Many live near, or even on top of, ancient sites that have a long history of Greek mythology. In the Aegean Sea, on the island of Mykonos, for example, children still hear stories about the hero Hercules, who is believed to be buried there. The elders also tell stories of Odysseus, the Ithacan king who traveled the oceans and had many fantastic adventures.

Most Greeks belong to the Greek Orthodox Church, which has many saints. Greeks pray regularly to their saints, especially in times of trouble.

In the Middle East, every country except Israel is primarily Islamic. That means most of the people are Muslims and follow the religion of Islam, which is based on the teachings of Muhammed as written in the holy book, the Koran. Muslim children learn their most basic family and community values from the Koran. This holy book is the basis of their religious, social, and cultural education. Through the Koran, Muslim children learn to obey their parents and to respect others.

Sharing Work and Fun

To manage housework and daily chores in European urban and suburban families, many parents have established divisions of labor that serve the family's needs for food, shelter, clothing, and love. For example, it is often the mother who cooks dinner, but it is her husband and children who clean up the house. The husband maintains the family car while the mother shops

＊ Crowned with flowers, dairy cows in the Swiss Alps are brought home from the pastures by the children of a family in the region of Vaud.

for the children's clothes. Daughters set the table for dinner while the sons take out the trash. In the evening, parents help with homework or read a book to younger children at bedtime.

In southern Spain, children are expected to contribute even more to the household chores. For example, daughters often do the shopping on Saturdays, carrying a straw basket from one store to the next, choosing the best breads, produce, and meats. These young girls use shopping skills taught to them at an early age by their mothers or grandmothers. In the afternoon, when their chores are done, many girls invite their friends over to visit and play. Boys often play soccer, one of the most popular sports in Spain and all of Europe. In southern Spain, children must find things to do indoors in the afternoons, since it is often too hot to play outside.

In other European countries, such as Norway, children also help their mothers with the shopping. This is because many families shop three or four times a week. They usually go to different shops on a daily basis to buy the things they need for that evening or the next day. To shop for dinner, a person may go to one shop that sells meat, another that sells fruits and vegetables, another for milk and cheese, a bakery for breads, and still another shop for pastries and candy for dessert. Although this method ensures freshness and variety, it is also time-consuming. Each shopping trip can take several hours.

In the Swiss Alps, one of the biggest jobs for a dairy family is getting the cows from their barns in the village to pastures in the mountains every spring. All the family members must get involved in this huge task. But sometimes they turn this job into a kind of sport. Because the cows often fight at this time of year, they are entered into competitions where they try to gore each other with their horns. Dairy families enjoy this game and are proud of their "queens," which is what they call the winners of the fights.

European families have many opportunities to have fun together. For example, they may take a day trip to the zoo, a carnival, a museum, or a park. During summer vacations, they may spend a month or two with relatives in the country or by the sea. This way, the elderly members of the family can spend more time with their grandchildren and parents can relax from the demands of work and full-time child care.

Much of Ireland is still rural and many people still work in farming professions. Along the rivers and coastline, fishing is important for both food and sport. Boys learn to fish just for fun when they are young, and, when they grow up, they often become professional fishermen. While the men are out fishing, their wives look after the home and children—picking the kids up at school, preparing a snack, helping them with their homework, and preparing the evening meal.

The Spanish Familia

Most people living in Spain are members of the Catholic Church, which has had a strong influence in this Mediterranean country for centuries. Because the Catholic Church discourages its members from using birth control, many have large families with many children. It is quite common for a Spanish family to have up to eight or ten children, which means lots of brothers and sisters to play with.

About one third of Spanish families live on farms, many of them in the wine country of southern Spain. In the middle of the day, all family members come home from work or school to have lunch together. This is the main meal of the day. The mother and grandmother (who often lives with the family or nearby) prepare the meal's many dishes, but everyone gets involved in bringing the food to the table. In the evening, around nine o'clock, they all have a light supper of fruit and cheese before getting ready for bed.

It is not always easy for the father to support his children. As is true of governments in many European countries, the Spanish government gives each family a certain amount of money every year to help provide for each child. In addition, as soon as the sons are old enough, they usually start to help their father on the farm. Daughters help with planting and harvesting, in addition to assisting their mother in the care of the house. This illustrates some of the advantages and disadvantages of having a large family: lots of help on the farm, but lots of mouths to feed.

Older children, especially the girls, help the mother take care of and sometimes raise the youngest children, especially the infants and toddlers. They may take the younger children to school and church. The parents also expect to be well taken care of when they are elderly. Many Spanish children are loyal to their parents, and believe it is their duty to care for them when they are in old age.

Throughout much of the United Kingdom—which includes England, Scotland, Northern Ireland, and Wales—families meet in the late afternoon for tea, especially on Sundays. Together, they drink tea and share delicious cakes, cookies, and other sweet desserts. At the same time, they share news, opinions, and gossip.

On most of the islands in Greece, many people still work as fishermen or sailors. The first-born son of each family is expected to follow in his father's footsteps and become a fisherman. He will inherit his father's or his grandfather's fishing boat when he grows up. In many Mediterranean villages, it is also the boys' job to keep the family's house sparkling white by painting the house with whitewash every month. The boys also learn important skills related to the sea, such as how to dive, how to catch octopuses, and how to find living sponges.

Caring for the Elderly

Once the children are grown, few European families live together under one roof. Young people often enter universities in the city and, once they get a job and marry, settle there or in a suburb. Older parents and grandparents often remain in their towns and villages far away. In Italy, for example, this distance may mean that older people maintain their family farm or vineyard by themselves. But children and grandchildren often leave the city to visit the family home on weekends and holidays.

Sometimes such distances between members can make caring for the elderly difficult. For example, a widower grandfather may live alone on the old family farm, where he continues to garden in order to provide for himself. When his family visits him on the weekends, they try to help as much as possible. Although many elderly have the option of moving in with their children and grandchildren, most prefer to live independently in their own homes.

With all of the memories of family gatherings that have taken place there, homes are very important centers of comfort to the elderly. They do not want to leave them just because they are old. If they have taken good care of themselves during their long lifetimes, many are able to continue living on their own. In fact, many older people like to prepare big traditional meals for their children and grandchildren when they come to visit from the big cities on weekends and holidays.

When an elderly parent or grandparent becomes unable to care for himself or herself, the children often decide among themselves who will take the older person into his or her home and provide the direct care. A daughter who does not work outside the home may volunteer for this responsibility. Or the best choice may be a family member who has an extra room or even a small apartment attached to the house. Sometimes, however, none of the children is able to properly take care of the elderly parent, and so he or she may go to live in a rest home or a nursing home, to be looked after by health-care professionals.

Families Change

Families have changed significantly in Europe and the Middle East in recent years. One of the main reasons for these changes is economic. Many European mothers and fathers work outside of the home and leave their children in public day-care centers during most weekday hours. But many governments have recognized how these long hours apart can affect family life. Sweden and Norway, for example, have developed special programs to allow parents to stay home with their children while being paid for a certain period of time off work.

In Eastern Europe and the countries of the former Soviet Union, family life is also changing fast. Under communism, most people did not have many options. They often had to live where the government allowed them to live and had to work in the few professions that were available. But now people, especially the younger generation, are making daily lifestyle and political decisions on their own. With the growth of freedom and democracy comes new personal responsibilities for the key elements of one's daily life.

5

Asia

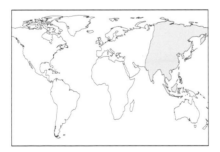

The huge continent of Asia extends from the Ural Mountains in Russia to the Arctic, Pacific, and Indian Oceans. Some of Asia's most economically vital islands include Japan, Taiwan, and Sri Lanka. China and India are the two largest countries. Southeast Asia includes Vietnam, Thailand, and Indonesia, while Korea and Hong Kong are part of East Asia.

For several thousand years, China, India, and Japan have developed unique and enduring cultures. While occasionally at war with each other, these societies more often have traded with each other and positively influenced each other's customs, traditions, languages, and religions. During this time, they and their neighbors have developed dynamic centers of trade and

✳ Opposite: A one-child Chinese family goes for a bicycle ride in Hohhot, Mongolia.

government, including the ancient Japanese city of Edo (now Tokyo), Ayuttaya in Thailand, Calcutta in India, and Peking (or Beijing) in China.

Beginning in the 1500s, many Asian countries were colonized by various powers, including England, France, Portugal, and the Netherlands. Asia's mostly tropical climate made it an ideal place to grow spices, coffee, tea, rubber, and other products that Europeans wanted but could not grow at home. India, Vietnam, Malaysia, Singapore, and Indonesia are among the countries that did not regain their independence until soon after World War II.

After a period of adjustment to this new independence, Asia has begun to take its place in the world as a powerful global economic power and important industrial region. Alongside the slower pace of traditional herding, fishing, and rice farming, today most Asian countries are in the midst of rapid economic growth and development. Every day, more and more Asian men and women work in industry and business as factory workers, engineers, and executives.

Caring for Children

In addition to its bustling cities, much of Asia has traditionally been influenced by rural and agricultural ways of life. Families have tended to be large, and children have been raised to work alongside their parents in rice paddies, pastures, and fishing boats. Today, as Asia becomes more industrialized and the importance of education has greatly increased, children are now encouraged to study and do homework rather than to toil at manual labor.

In the more modern sectors of Asian society, some parents clearly divide professional and child-raising responsibilities. In Japan, most middle-class fathers tend to spend long days and evenings at the office, while mothers devote their full time to children's care and education. This almost complete division of labor affects the family in many ways. For one, it means that children spend little time with their fathers and are disciplined

✳ A large Nepali family gathers for a portrait outside its home in the Himalayas, near Pokhara.

mostly by their mothers. Since one's appearance is very important in Japanese society, mothers often pay extra attention to how their children appear to their schoolmates. This may even include what a child's school lunch looks like. In order to compete with other children, each meal must be not only nutritious but fun to look at, so the child does not become an outcast and ridiculed. One popular treat is white rice balls decorated with diced vegetables arranged to look like a friendly face.

Some rural and mountain families, as in Tibet and Nepal, arrange their children's marriages when the children are still quite young. At that time, the boy's family may promise a marriage price and the girl's family may pledge a smaller dowry than if the girl were older. The typical engagement period can last a long time, in part because girls often don't want to leave their parental homes. Sometimes the parents are reluctant to give up their daughters because they help with the family's workload and contribute to its income.

In many Hindu households in India, parents believe it is their responsibility to adjust to their child's world, especially their son's. Because their children may fall ill and die in their early years, parents tend to indulge each child in the hope that he or she will survive. In the Ongee community on the Little Andaman Island in India's Bay of Bengal, for example, both men and women devote themselves fully to their children's care and education, from infancy onward.

Like many Chinese and other Indian children who grow up in extended families, Ongee children learn to live with numerous adult male and female role models. Unlike many Japanese families, where the father works long hours and leaves much of the childrearing to the mother, Ongee children are raised with an equal amount of attention from both parents and all the adults in their campsite. Child care is seen as an activity in which all adults are keen on getting involved.

Families Teach Values

One family value that is becoming increasingly common throughout Asia, particularly in the cities and outlying suburbs, is the importance of education and financial success. Many families now follow a daily schedule that revolves to a large extent around the children's schoolwork. Passing from one grade to the next can be quite competitive, as on the small but prosperous island nation of Singapore, where the majority of the population is of Chinese origin.

A family in Singapore may be deeply ashamed if its children do not do well in school or become successful after graduation. A child is expected to succeed not only for himself or herself, but for the entire family. In Singapore, selfishness is strongly discouraged, as it is in most other Asian families.

In the rougher world of Asian rural and mountain life, a family's values often have more to do with its members' very survival. For example, Ongee men teach their sons how to be brave and to hunt well. Boys are also taught not to cry, since the Ongee believe that only women should reveal sad feelings.

✳ A father holds his son as he instructs him in how to perform an incense ritual at a Buddhist temple in Hangzhou, Zhejiang Province, China.

During a time of mourning, women and girls do most of the crying for the entire family. The men believe that if a man sheds tears, he will "fail as a hunter."

Sharing Work and Fun

The growing emphasis on education means many rural and middle-class Asian children spend more time with homework than housework. In urban families in Hong Kong, children have little time to help around the house, because they are commonly given a great deal of schoolwork. Hong Kong parents hope their children will do well in school and get jobs that make them financially successful. Once they get a good education, few Asian children want to stay on their family farms or in rural areas. Instead, they choose to find work in business and markets of the big cities.

Other Asian families, especially those in mountain regions, continue to practice the most traditional family divisions of labor. In farming communities, all capable family members must work in the fields during the spring planting season and fall harvest.

The Bhotia people, who live in Nepal, combine a nomadic herding life with business and farming. A typical Bhotia family brings all relatives into one household. Whether they're herding yaks, or selling homemade products, each Bhotia family relies entirely on its own members, rather than

✳ A Singapore family gathers together for dinner as the eldest daughter finishes her schoolwork at the table.

* Nomadic women and children sit in their camp in the Kulu Valley, in the northern region of India.

on the rest of the community, for its own survival. Bhotia children must help with daily chores, such as fetching water and spinning wool. Boys learn how to herd and lasso the family's yaks, and girls learn how to roast and grind barley and make butter and cheese.

Mechanized rice planters have relieved many Japanese farm families of the hard work of planting and harvesting rice in wet rice paddies from dawn to dusk. But women in these families often do most of the other work, such as caring for the family pigs. They also rely on their female relatives living nearby—especially grandmothers, mothers, and sisters—to lend them emotional and material support. Because the men do not participate much in raising the children, most boys and girls spend huge amounts of time only in the company of women.

Ongee children refer to all adult males as *omoree*, or "father." Ongee fathers play ruggedly with their children to make them physically fit and to help them learn to compete. Later, the children will follow the men into the forest to hunt wild pigs. While the older boys watch the men hunt, the younger children learn about the edible plants in the area. Back at the campsite, the women take the girls to catch fish with small hand nets, and show them how to snatch crabs when the ocean tide recedes. Later in the day, men, women, and children will often collect firewood and drinking water together. This way, everybody in the family teaches the children about the island's resources and how to use them.

In addition to their studies, Asian children like to have fun, as do all other children around the world. Chinese children may attend religious festivals that include outdoor puppet shows, or they may watch a noisy and colorful parade filled with fireworks that celebrates a new year. In between chores, many Bhotia children find time to play games, including hopscotch and marbles. Children in Singapore and Malaysia play a billiards-like game called *caroms*, in which players try to knock checker-like pieces into holes at the corners of a playing board. Playing and celebrating together, like working together, can help families reinforce their sense of being a group.

Caring for the Elderly

In China, the mother is often considered the "glue" that binds a family together. As in all families, the Chinese have a tradition of strong bonds between a mother and her children. When a Chinese woman becomes too old to care for herself, she knows that her children, both sons and daughters, will remember her devotion and, in turn, will provide for her. This may mean she will leave her own home to live with her children, or that they will help her remain independent by spending a lot of time cooking and cleaning for her.

Japanese parents also tend to devote much of their adult lives to their children's education and personal development. In response to this love and caring, sons and daughters often adopt a profound sense of obligation to their parents. When parents become elderly, their grown children take them into their homes and care for them until they pass away. The family emphasis on education and financial success often pays off as parents get old, since their children are better able to care and provide for a larger family.

The profound sense of obligation to one's parents and elderly family members goes on even after those members die. Many Chinese families honor the memory of a deceased ancestor by lighting sticks of incense every day and placing them by a photograph of the dead person. In addition, they pray regularly at Buddhist and other religious temples, asking for blessings for family members who have died.

Families Change

Since the early 1960s, many regions in Asia have experienced great economic and political changes. Many countries began by providing skilled and inexpensive labor to North American and European manufacturing companies. Today, thanks to an emphasis on education for their workers, these countries have become powerful industrial societies themselves.

✳ Members of a Hong Kong family bring gifts to a grave in order to honor the memory of a loved one.

Industrialization has encouraged the growth of a middle class whose lifestyle is gradually replacing the traditionally rural ways. Such economic and political changes have had a dramatic impact on traditional family life in Asia. For example, many young adults now earn enough money to reject the traditional practice of living under the same roof as other family members. Plus, more and more women are taking positions in the workplace and leaving child care to grandparents and professional day-care facilities.

In Japan, children have traditionally not been encouraged to express their own feelings and opinions. This has been discouraged for the sake of social etiquette, group and family harmony, and "status." But now, as industrialization progresses and cultures are more in contact with each other, many Japanese young people are learning the American and European practice of encouraging self-expression. This influence has caused many young Japanese to resist many of Japan's traditional social pressures and insistence on conformity.

Another change in Asia—in China, for example—is in what ways society views the differences between boys and girls.

✳ Seamstresses work diligently at a clothing factory in Kowloon, Hong Kong.

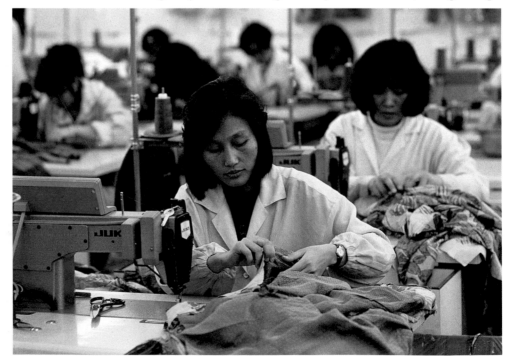

＊ A Japanese father keeps a watchful eye on his son as he does his homework on Honshu Island.

Traditionally, boys have been preferred to girls, in great part
because China's roots are agrarian and because men have held
most of the economic and social power. These attitudes have
also meant that boys received more attention and more encour-
agement to study and succeed. Today, though, that attitude is
changing, and girls are also learning to develop their skills and
talents outside the home. With this change, many young
Chinese women are also entering professional areas once
reserved strictly for men. These changes will definitely affect
the basic structure and traditions of the family in Asia, just as
families changed in the United States when women entered the
workforce in great numbers. Just how these similar circumstances will alter the various societies in Asia, however, still
remains to be seen.

6

$\mathcal{A}$ ustralia and the South Pacific

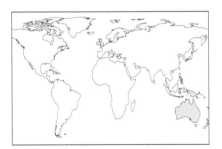

Australia, New Zealand, and Papua New Guinea are the largest countries in the South Pacific region, which includes Micronesia, Fiji, and the Solomon Islands, among others. Some residents are descended from English-speaking immigrants, but many are indigenous tribes that have lived in this area for centuries.

Eleven times the size of Texas, Australia is the smallest of Earth's continents. Australia also has one of the highest standards of living and literacy rates in the world. Although the continent was colonized by British prisoners in the early nineteenth century, many others, especially Chinese and Europeans,

65

＊ Opposite: An Aborigine father and son pose together in Australia's Northern Territory.

have immigrated since World War II. Most Australians today work in manufacturing, farming, or raising livestock—mostly cattle and sheep.

As settlements of immigrants have grown over the past 150 years, the number of native peoples, or Aborigines, has diminished. Today, the remaining 150,000 Aborigines—including the Tiwi of northern Australia—often face discrimination by other Australians as they struggle to maintain their traditional values and customs.

New Zealand, an independent nation east of Australia, was also settled by English-speaking immigrants in the 1800s. New Zealand also has a large population of indigenous people—Maori—who migrated from Polynesia more than 1,000 years ago. Most New Zealanders raise sheep and make dairy products, such as butter and cheese, for a living.

As the eastern half of a large island in the South Pacific Ocean, Papua New Guinea was a part of Australia until the small nation gained its independence in 1975. The country of Papua New Guinea is made up of more than 600 islands, with 4 million people and 750 languages and dialects. Because the region is rugged and very mountainous, with many volcanos, some tribal groups have little contact with each other and the outside world. This isolation has allowed them to retain their traditional practices for thousands of years.

Caring for Children

On the tiny island of Ifalik, part of the Federated States of Micronesia in the South Pacific, the people say that each baby born is a "king." Most men on the island are doting fathers, but because the Ifalik community practices polygyny, the more wives and children a man has, the less time he has to spend with each branch of his large family.

Among the Tiwi of northern Australia, a man may also have several wives. In addition, all children in a given camp are considered "siblings," all adults are considered "mothers" or "fathers." While the young children often stay close to their biological mothers and fathers, they also have many other "parents" who carry, feed, and play with them.

Tiwi children are rarely disciplined. This is because their parents consider experience to be the best teacher, rather than warnings and admonishments. The Tiwi expect their children to learn how to swim and climb trees, for example, by imitation rather than by direct teaching.

Tiwi fathers choose husbands for their daughters when the girls are quite young, sometimes in their early teens. The daughter then joins her husband's family and promises to serve him as well as his other wives, if he has any. If her husband dies, it is common for his brother to then marry her right away.

Among the Huli people of central Papua New Guinea, married couples often live apart. A husband may live with his father and a wife with her sisters. The children live primarily with their mothers. When a boy reaches the age of seven, he often leaves his mother's house to live with his father. That way he can learn the many skills he will need to become a man.

Teaching Values to the Young

Tiwi parents often teach their children values through traditional beliefs that have been part of their culture for centuries. For example, the Tiwi believe that if a person wastes food, he or she will soon be bitten by a poisonous snake or crocodile. By fearing such an eventuality, Tiwi children learn the importance of respecting their food supply and natural resources.

Tiwi boys and girls are also encouraged to develop themselves as individuals. Personal achievement is an important Tiwi value. Each person is considered first a unique being and second a member of the community. For example, a woman is judged on how well she can provide food for her family. A man can show his achievements by composing poetry, dancing, painting, and carving. However, men and women have equal say in most family decisions.

Huli children learn the critical importance of raising pigs for their families' survival. A man's wealth and status in his clan is based on how many pigs he owns. However, the pigs are kept in the women's houses so they can be cared for.

Among the different groups who live in Papua New Guinea's Sepik River Valley, including the Huli, children hear many stories about magic and spirits from older family members as they sit around their campfires at night. Many of these unique stories involve crocodiles, since it is believed that the crocodile is the originator of Earth and the creator of the people.

Sharing Work and Fun

The descendants of Australia's immigrants often live according to the same social structures and rules as their European relations. Nuclear families consisting of two parents and several children commonly live together under one roof. During the day, most children attend school while their parents work. After school, boys often play soccer or cricket (a baseball-like team sport of English origin) while girls play volleyball.

In the evening, many Australian children are expected to help their parents, either by preparing dinner or cleaning up after the meal is finished. Later, the children may do their homework or watch television. For fun on the weekends, some families like to visit Australia's many dramatic caves, go bowling, or shop at the mall in a big city like Sydney or Melbourne.

When Tiwi mothers and fathers go into the bush to hunt opossums, snakes, crocodiles, and the rat-like bandicoot, their sons and daughters often go along with them. On these excursions, the children are encouraged to kill small animals and contribute to the family's food supply. While men and women share most of the hunting and gathering, the women are also responsible for making tools and containers, gathering water, and carrying fire from one camp to another. (If the cooking fire goes out in one camp, fire is carried from another camp to light it.)

Among the Ifalik, the women plant, harvest, and cook taro, a tropical plant that most local people eat. While the men do all the fishing, most of their children's food comes from other members of their fathers' households. Because they are not

✳ An Australian family plays cricket together in Australia's Northern Territory.

expected to work as much, and because they receive tributes from other tribal members, Ifalik chiefs and their wives often have more free time to spend with their children.

From their mothers, Huli girls learn the skills they will need as adults and mothers. For centuries, children in the Sepik River Valley have been expected to pluck the chickens that are killed that day, and to prepare the fish that has been caught that morning. Recently, however, many of these children have begun to attend school and learn how to read and write. Their new responsibilities mean children are not expected to do as much domestic work as in the past.

Sepik River Valley families often hold a Sing Sing to celebrate events such as a birth or death, a marriage or harvest, or the passing from childhood to adulthood. Family and village members dress up in grass skirts, shell and bead necklaces, and put bird feathers in their headpieces—to these people, birds symbolize good luck and protection from the enemy.

Caring for the Elderly

One reason Tiwi men marry several women is so at least one wife may survive to take care of him when he is old. But if an old person is left without any immediate family to take care of him or her, the family of a sibling is obligated to be the primary caregiver.

Traditionally, as a Tiwi woman ages, her power and prestige also increase. Her age gives her the right to direct her husband's other wives in their activities. Eventually, she becomes the "supreme" mother of both her daughters and her co-wives' daughters. While her sons look after and care for her, they also seek her advice and counsel. Like many Asian cultures, the Tiwi also have daily practices that honor their dead. One such practice is painting their ancestors' skulls and bones and keeping them in a special place.

Families Change

As societies are exposed to new influences, they often decide to change their traditional beliefs and practices. The traditional practice of polygyny among the Tiwi, for example, has become

✳ Three generations of a Maori family enjoy a visit at a hospital in Te Puia Springs, North Island, New Zealand.

✳ A Huli father poses with his four wives and children outside their home in central Papua New Guinea.

less common. For decades, Catholic missionaries have condemned the practice of having more than one wife and of allowing young girls to marry much older men. As a result, some Tiwi have begun to phase out polygyny and to allow girls to marry whomever and whenever they wish.

In recent years, many Tiwi have been moved from their residential areas to settlements where they are now taken care of by the Australian government. Such changes have had an important impact on the Tiwi family structure—particularly on the status and power of older women. Whereas in the past, family members relied on the hard-earned wisdom and advice of these matriarchs, government administrators are now taking over that role, training young Tiwi to live according to Western rather than indigenous traditions. Despite such changes—including the more widespread introduction of Western values—many Tiwi have begun to adapt and blend their old ways of life with the new. They believe that the survival of individual Tiwi is more important in the long term than the survival of a certain way of life.

Conclusion:
The Human Family

Families around the world may vary in size, domestic arrangement, languages, and customs, but they also share many basic ideals and functions.

Regardless of where they are on the Earth, families raise their children in hopes that their young will become caring and responsible members of their communities. In the rain forests of South America, this may mean sharing the meat after a successful hunt. In the cities of Europe, this may mean working with school teachers to improve the quality of education. In farming communities of Asia, this may mean respecting one's elders, using the proper forms of speech to address older people.

Families also try to pass on their values to the young. Family values are usually rooted in cultural traditions and religious practices. In Christian, Jewish, Muslim, Buddhist, and many other communities, parents will take their children to places of worship to be exposed to those teachings. In hunter-gatherer societies, children listen to stories told by their elders about how their people came to be, and how the younger generations are expected to behave.

All families also work together in one way or another, whether they are in the mountainous pastoral and agricultural communities of Tibet or on the green and grassy savannas of Africa. In industrialized communities, families work together in specialized ways—on projects around the house or on projects for their community. And part of working together is playing together, as families do in the wine villages of southern Spain and the rain-forest hamlets of the South Pacific. In some cases, without these kinds of cooperation and harmony, a family may not survive.

In the industrialized communities of Europe, America, and Canada, for example, the elderly may receive money from the government or from their investments. This may allow them to continue to live independently. When they become too frail to care for themselves, they may go to live with a child, or they may have health-care professionals take care of their needs.

No matter what their structure or environment, families all around the world help their members to grow and become productive individuals. For most people, families provide the single most important source of care and comfort—the foundations needed for a happy, healthy, and productive life. The fact that all humans need families brings countries and cultures together in a fundamental way. And in this way, we all become part of one big human family, caring, working, and having fun together, no matter where we are.

Glossary

acculturation The process of learning or incorporating another culture through direct contact.

apartheid An official policy in South Africa that separated the white, black, and "coloured" (mixed race and other races, such as Indian) populations. When in force, this policy promoted the supremacy of whites in all areas of society. Apartheid was abolished in South Africa in 1993.

ethnic Pertaining to a specific religious, racial, national, or cultural group, or combination thereof.

hunter-gatherer One who relies on hunting and gathering as a primary method for survival. In hunter-gatherer groups, the men usually hunt animals and the women gather plant products for food and medicine.

indigenous People, animals, and plants that exist in an area for a long time. Native Americans are indigenous because they lived on the North American continent for thousands of years before the Europeans arrived. However, their ancestors immigrated to the Americas at least 15,000 years ago.

industrial Pertaining to a way of life that places an emphasis on industry. An industrialized region or nation often mass-produces or manufactures the items needed by its population, such as food, clothing, housing, and furniture.

kibbutz A collective farm or settlement in Israel.

kinship A system of family relationships, including genetic, marital, and, occasionally, fictional relationships.

nomads People who move from place to place seasonally in search of food and water for themselves or the animals they herd.

pastoralists People who support themselves by herding animals, primarily cattle, goats, and sheep.

polyandry The practice of having more than one husband at a time.

polygamy The practice of having more than one wife or husband at a time.

polygyny The practice of having more than one wife at a time.

savanna A flat, treeless grassland of tropical and subtropical regions.

tribe A group of people whose members share a common ancestry, language, culture, and name.

tundra A treeless area found in arctic and high-altitude regions.

yak A long-haired, cattle-like animal that lives in the mountains of Central Asia. Yaks are often domesticated for use by the people of this region.

Further Reading

Boy Scouts of America Staff. *Family Life*. Irving, TX: Boy Scouts of America, 1991.

Cline, Ruth K. *Focus on Families: A Reference Handbook*. Santa Barbara, CA: ABC-CLIO, Inc., 1989.

Cooney, Caroline B. *Family Reunion*. New York: Bantam, 1989.

Glotzbach, Gerri, et al. *The Family*. Vero Beach, FL: Rourke, 1990.

Hautzig, Esther. *Endless Steppe: Growing Up in Siberia*. New York: HarperCollins Children's Books, 1992.

Hodges, Margaret. *Making a Difference: The Story of an American Family*. New York: Macmillan Children's Book Group, 1989.

Holland, Gini. *Ireland Is My Home*. Milwaukee, WI: Gareth Stevens Publications, 1993. (This multibook series focuses on family life in many different countries.)

Jenness, Aylette. *Families: A Celebration of Diversity, Commitment, and Love*. Boston: Houghton Mifflin, 1990.

Schachtman, Tom. *Growing Up Masai*. New York: Macmillan, 1981.

Vaughan, Jenny. *Families Around the World*. Minneapolis, MN: Lerner Publications, 1986.

Wilkins, Frances. *Family Life from Nineteen Thirty to the Nineteen Eighties*. North Pomfret, VT: Trafalgar, 1986.

Wolf, Bernard. *In the Year of the Tiger*. New York: Macmillan, 1988.

Index

Photo Credits